STEP-by-STEP

SCIENCE

Sound

Helena Ramsay

Illustrated by Pat Tourret and Andrew Farmer

CHILDREN'S PRESS®

A Division of Grolier Publishing

NEW YORK • LONDON • HONG KONG • SYDNEY
DANBURY, CONNECTICUT

Photographs: James Davis Travel Photography: page 14; Mary Evans Picture Library:
page 7, left, 21; Greg Evans: page 26, right; Eye Ubiquitous: page 18 (Skjold), 22 (T. Nottingham);
Sally and Richard Greenhill Photo Library: page 19 (Sally Greenhill); Robert Harding Picture Library:
page 29; Hutchison: page 28, right; Image Bank: page 12, 26, left; Oxford Scientific Films: page 6 (Raj
Kamal), 16 (Stephen Dalton), 23 (R. Van Nostrand), 25 (K. G. Vock Okapia), 30, bottom (Michael
Fogden), 31 (Tom Ulrich); Photostage: page 11 (Donald Cooper); Redferns: page 10 (David Redfern);
Science Photo Library: page 9 (David Parker), 13 (NASA), 17 (Yves Baulieu Publiphoto Diffusion);
South American Pictures: page 8 (Jason P. Howe); Tony Stone Worldwide:
page 5, both, 7, 10, 15, 24, 27, 28 (left), 30, top; Zefa: cover.

Planning and production by Discovery Books Limited
Design: Ian Winton
Consultant: Chris Oxlade

Visit Children's Press on the Internet at:
http://publishing.grolier.com

First published in 1998 by Franklin Watts

First American edition 1998 by Children's Press

ISBN: 0-516-20958-2
A CIP catalog record
for this book is available from
the Library of Congress

Copyright © Franklin Watts 1998

Printed in Dubai

Contents

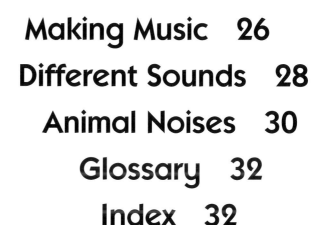

A Noisy World

Sit still and listen. How many different sounds can you hear? Can you hear the wind rustling the leaves of the trees or the sound of birds singing? Perhaps you can hear the sound of traffic or the roar of an airplane in the sky above you.

Some sounds are nice. We usually enjoy listening to music or the sound of waves crashing onto the shore.

Other sounds are not so nice. We often call these unpleasant sounds "noises." A road drill makes a loud noise, and so does a heavy truck or an airplane.

Loud and Quiet

Where are there more sounds — in the city or in the countryside? Wherever we go there are always sounds of some kind, even if they are very quiet sounds.

The farther away you get from the thing that is making the sound, the quieter the sound becomes. This is because the sound spreads through the air. The closer you get to the thing that is making the sound, the louder it seems.

We can hear loud sounds from a long way off. But we have to get very close and listen carefully to quiet things to hear them properly. If we move away from a quiet sound, we may not be able to hear it at all.

The loudest sound ever heard on Earth was made when a volcano erupted on Krakatoa, a tiny island in Southeast Asia. The eruption took place in 1883, and the noise could be heard 1,863 miles (3,000 kilometers) away.

Sound Waves

If you pluck the string of a guitar you can see it **vibrating** as it produces a musical note. Every sound we hear is made by something vibrating.

The air around us is made up of tiny parts called **particles**. When a thing vibrates, it makes the particles in the air vibrate, too.

As they vibrate, the particles bump into the particles next to them. In this way, the sound travels through the air in waves.

Oscilloscope

A machine called an oscilloscope allows us to see sound waves on a screen.

HOW SOUND TRAVELS

This activity will help you to understand how sound moves through the air. You will need a set of dominoes.

1. Stand the dominoes on their ends in a straight line.

2. Push the domino at one end of the line over. In turn, all the other dominoes will fall over. This movement is similar to the way that sound vibrations travel through the air.

Voices

The sound of your voice is made by vibrations in your throat. We use our voices every day to talk to one another.

We also use our voices for singing, laughing, and crying.

When you speak, air passes over two flaps of skin in your throat called your **vocal cords**. The air makes them vibrate and produce sound.

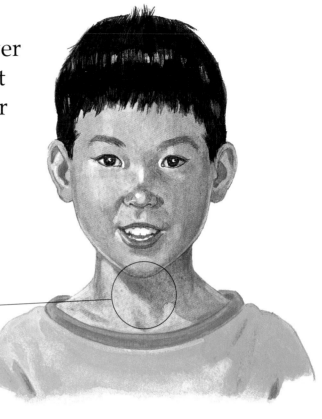

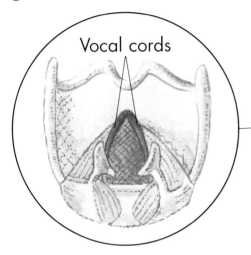

Vocal cords

Try talking while you hold your throat gently with your finger and thumb. You will be able to feel the vibrations. The sounds made by your vocal cords are shaped into words by your tongue, lips, teeth, and jaw.

Opera Singer

This opera singer can fill a concert hall with her voice. She has learned to use certain muscles in her body to help control the flow of air from her lungs over her vocal cords.

The Speed of Sound

Sound moves quickly through the air. It takes only three seconds for sound to travel half a mile (1 km). Light moves much faster than sound. In three seconds it can travel nearly 621,000 miles (1 million km).

As light moves faster than sound, we see a flash of lightning during a storm before we hear the thunder.

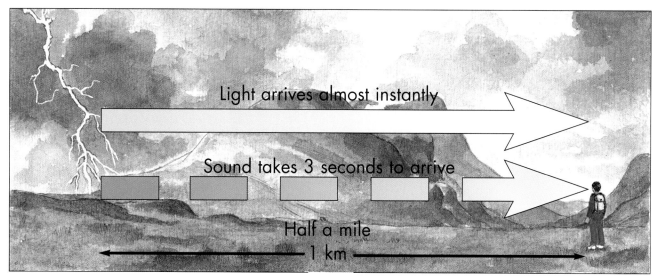

Light arrives almost instantly

Sound takes 3 seconds to arrive

Half a mile
1 km

SIGHT AND SOUND

1. Go outside and ask a friend to walk about 300 feet (100 meters) away from you.

2. When you are facing each other, ask your friend to clap.

There will be a fraction of a second between the moment that you see her clap and when you actually hear the sound of her clapping. This is the time that it takes for the sound to travel through the air to your ears.

Silence in Space

These two astronauts cannot speak normally to each other. This is because there is no air in space for sound waves to travel through.

Sound on the Move

How fast sound travels depends on what it is traveling through. If the particles of the substance are close together, the sound waves will travel faster.

GAS

LIQUID

SOLID

Particles in a liquid, like water, are closer together than particles in a gas, like air.

The particles in a solid object are packed very tightly together. When they vibrate, the particles bump into each other like people in a crowded room. Sound waves travel much more quickly through solids than through anything else.

Dolphins

Dolphins use sounds to communicate with each other under the water.

MAKE YOUR OWN TELEPHONE

1. Ask an adult to make small holes in the bottoms of two polystyrene cups.

2. Poke the ends of some string through the holes in each cup and secure it with a knot.

3. Ask a friend to hold one of the cups. Walk away holding the other cup until the string is tight.

4. Put the cup over one ear. When your friend talks, the sound vibrations should travel down the string to your ear.

Bouncing Back

When sound waves in the air or a liquid hit a solid object, parts of each wave bounce off. If you shout at a brick wall your voice comes bouncing back to you as an **echo**.

Bats, which fly around in the dark, use sound, not sight, to find their way around. A bat makes its own noises and listens to the echoes coming back from the objects all around it.

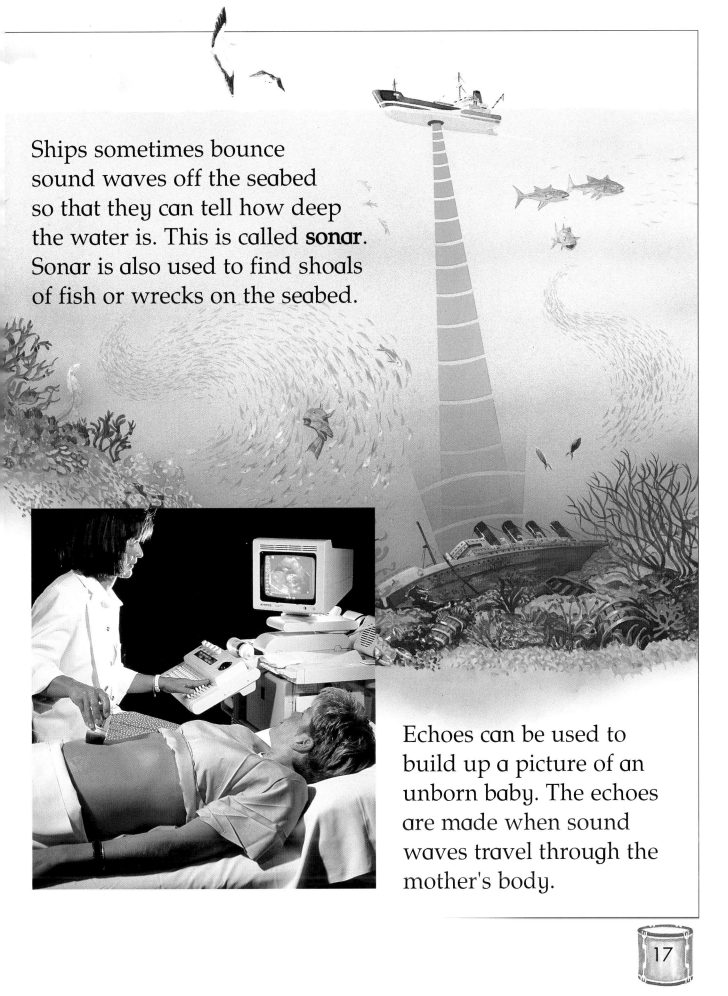

Ships sometimes bounce sound waves off the seabed so that they can tell how deep the water is. This is called **sonar**. Sonar is also used to find shoals of fish or wrecks on the seabed.

Echoes can be used to build up a picture of an unborn baby. The echoes are made when sound waves travel through the mother's body.

How We Hear

We use our ears and our brains to hear. The outer parts of the ears are like funnels for collecting sounds. Inside the ear there is a very thin piece of skin stretched tightly across a tube. This skin is called the **eardrum**.

The eardrum

The nerves to the brain

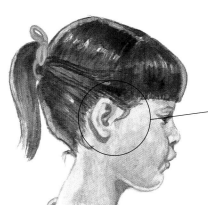

Even the tiniest sound wave makes the eardrum vibrate. The vibrations are passed through the different parts of the ear and turned into messages that pass along our **nerves** to our brains.

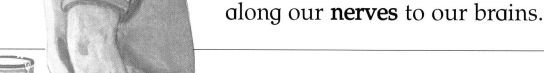

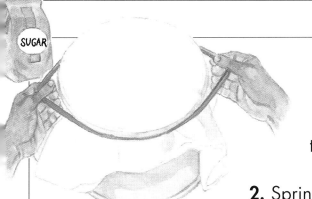

VIBRATING SOUND WAVES

1. Stretch a plastic bag tightly over a cake tin. Secure it with rubber bands to make a drum.

2. Sprinkle a teaspoonful of sugar onto your drum.

3. Hold a metal baking tray above the drum and beat it with a spoon. This makes the tray vibrate.

The vibrating air particles make the plastic on the drum vibrate just like the skin of a real eardrum. This makes the grains of sugar dance around.

Hearing Aid

Some people with poor hearing wear hearing aids. A hearing aid **amplifies** the sound, making it louder.

Make It Loud

Have you ever cupped your hands around your mouth and shouted to someone a long way off?

Sound waves lose energy as they spread out through the air. By cupping your hands around your mouth you can stop the waves from spreading out as much in the air.

When we want to listen to a distant sound we sometimes cup our hands behind our ears.

By cupping our hands behind our ears we catch more of the sound waves.

When we don't cup our hands behind our ears, we catch less of the sound waves.

AHOY THERE!

A bullhorn works in the same way as your cupped hands. An ear trumpet works in the same way as cupping your hands behind your ears.

1. Make two cone shapes from oaktag and sticky tape. Give one cone to a friend.

2. Walk in opposite directions until you can hardly hear each other when talking normally.

3. Try talking normally into the bullhorn while your friend listens through the ear trumpet. Can your friend hear you better?

Before hearing aids were invented, people with poor hearing used ear trumpets like this one.

Big Ears

Many animals depend on their sense of hearing for survival. The rabbit has large ears, which work like the ear trumpet on page 21. They catch more sound waves and allow the rabbit to hear a **predator** approaching and make its escape.

Owls have disks on their heads that help to direct sound into their large ears. An owl's hearing is so good that it can catch its **prey** in complete darkness.

Fennec Fox

The fennec fox lives on the grasslands of Africa. It uses its huge ears to hear insects moving under the ground. It then digs them up and eats them.

Where Does It Come From?

Have you ever wondered why we have two ears?

It is so that we can tell from which direction a sound is coming. Unless the sound is coming from directly in front or behind you, one ear will always hear it just before the other.

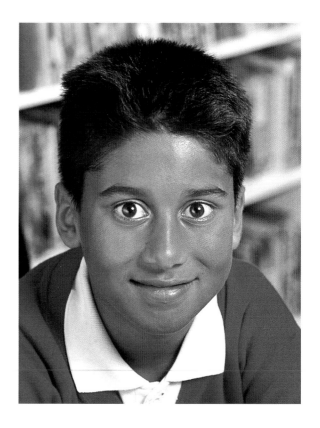

From the right

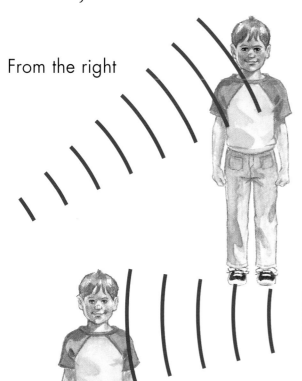

From the front

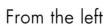

From the left

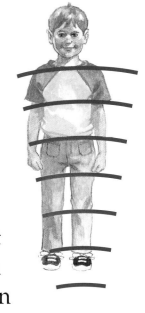

Our brains use the different messages coming from each ear to work out the direction of the sound.

24

WHICH DIRECTION?

This game can be played by four or five people.

1. One person should be blindfolded and sit in the center of a circle made by the others.

2. Each person, in turn, should make a soft sound. The blindfolded person should point to where he or she thinks the sound is coming from.

3. When each person has had a chance at being blindfolded, you can decide whose ears have the best sense of direction!

Not all creatures have ears on their heads. A toad's eardrum looks like a circle of skin, just behind its eye.

Making Music

There are many different kinds of musical instruments, and they all make the air vibrate in different ways.

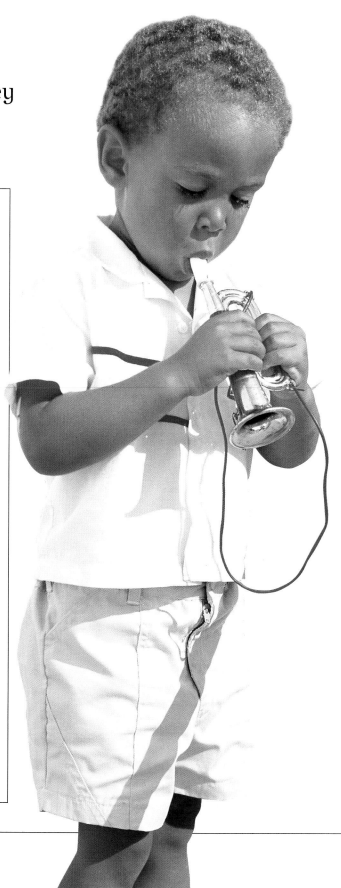

Rock 'n' Roll

This musician is using electrical amplifiers to make the sound of his guitar louder.

Drums are some of the oldest and simplest musical instruments in the world. All types of drums are made by stretching a tight skin across a frame. When the skin is struck, it vibrates, making the air both inside and outside the drum vibrate, too.

Different Sounds

Stringed instruments, like this harp, make sounds using vibrating strings.

The strings make very little sound on their own. The hollow body of the instrument picks up the sounds made by the strings and amplifies them.

This violin player is pressing her fingers down on the strings. In this way she makes the string she is playing shorter or longer. The short strings make high notes and the longer ones make low notes. The violin vibrates, making the sound louder.

Musical instruments like oboes, clarinets, and recorders are made of a pipe. The air trapped inside the pipe vibrates and makes a sound. A short pipe makes a higher sound than a long one.

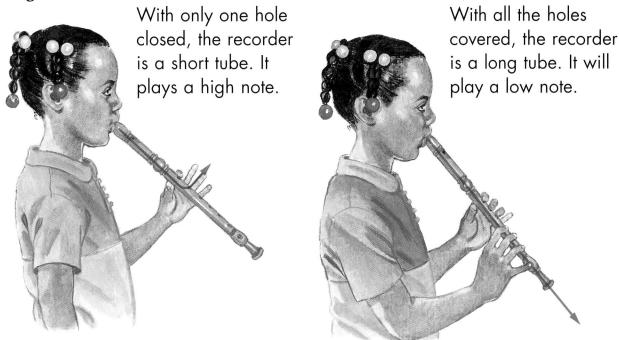

With only one hole closed, the recorder is a short tube. It plays a high note.

With all the holes covered, the recorder is a long tube. It will play a low note.

Some of these recorder players are making high sounds and others are making lower sounds.

Animal Noises

Many animals use sound to send messages to each other. The songs of male birds often send out two messages at once. They attract a female and warn off other males. Young birds call to their parents when they are hungry.

Croaking Frog

Frogs have air sacs in their throats. These act like the body of a musical instrument, making the frogs' croaking louder.

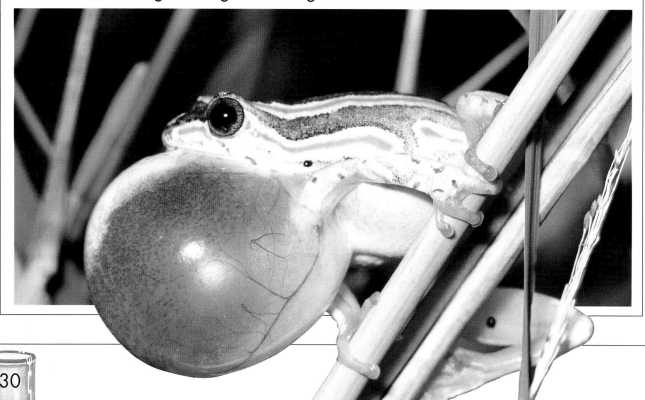

Rattlesnake

The rattlesnake makes a dry, rattling sound by shaking its tail. This sound warns people and animals to keep out of its way.

Animals can use sound to warn one another of danger. If a prairie dog sees an enemy approaching, it barks to tell the others in the pack to hide.

Glossary

Amplifies: Makes louder

Eardrum: A piece of stretched skin inside the ear, which vibrates when sound waves hit it

Echo: Sound waves that bounce back off a solid object

Nerves: Tiny bands of tissue all over the body that pass messages from the body to the brain

Particles: The tiny parts that everything is made of

Predator: An animal that kills and eats other animals

Prey: Animal hunted or killed by other animals for food

Sonar: A way of bouncing sound waves off objects under the water in order to find out where they are

Vibrating: Moving backward and forward very quickly

Vocal cords: flaps of skin in the throat, which vibrate to make sounds

Index